LAUGH LINES

A Dose of Humor,
A Dash of Angst

And Other Things
To Crease Your Face

By Linda D. Coker

First Edition October 2008

ISBN 978-0-615-25703-7

♥

Dedicated to my precious parents,
Jerry and Billie Brumbelow.
Thank you for being my greatest fans!
Your love and encouragement
mean everything to me.

♥

♥ Contents ♥

Nature

The Man In The Moon Has The Mumps

The oddest thing has happened,
And I hardly know what to say,
The man in the moon has come down with the mumps
And he cannot come out today.

I thought the moon looked different,
But I just couldn't place the change.
Now that I've learned the incredible truth,
I confess it is mighty strange.

He must have breathed bad space dust,
Or inhaled some space debris.
With tons and tons of galactical trash,
The universe must not be germ-free.

Yet the moon's not dark this evening.
It has a unique flair and whirl.
For during his recuperation, this week
That one in the moon is a girl.

Iris

There once was a flower named Iris,
Quite madly in love with Papyrus.
It must have been Fate,
That these two should mate:
Scented paper today doth inspire us!

Suncerity

A true-blue sun pupil I'm not:
I bask just until I'm too hot.
So, dripping with lotion
Applied with devotion
I'm covered, rays, take your best shot.

Dawn

The Fingers of Day reach far and wide
As Dawn brings forth Her Light,
And when They reach the other side
The Day gives way to Night.

Windrest
(A Japanese poetry form called Tonka)

Where does the wind rest
To gather its strength again?
In secluded caves,
Or high atop leafy trees
To start afresh as a breeze?

Autumn
(Haiku)

Leaves crimson, gold, brown
Celebrating the harvest
Fall like confetti

Dry Heat

It takes all I've got just to wake up
And whatever's left to arise.
I drag my legs over the edge of the bed
And attempt to pry open my eyes.

Nausea rolls deep in my stomach,
My head feels quite dull, numb and thick.
I'm planted in front of the AC,
Determined I shall not be sick.

It's not West Nile or a hangover,
That's bringing me straight to my knees.
It's surviving an Arizona summer,
At one hundred and fifteen degrees!

A Torrid Peace

Another torrid, blistering day
One hundred and twelve at least
When the power shut down
Right in the middle
Of cooking my evening feast.

Don't panic-don't worry-no sweat, I thought
Though sweat was already present
Take the food from the oven
Don't open the fridge
And then, just try to be patient.

I tried to dwell on various ways
To keep myself calm, dry and cool
I changed immediately
Into my suit and
I lounged in my turquoise blue pool.

And what a delicious wait it was
For the restart of the power!
No radios, motors,
AC hum or buzz
In two serenely sweet hours.

Although my day had started out
As a foul and blistering scorcher
Such peace in pure and
Liquid form changed it
From one hateful epoch of torture.

Eclipse

Tonight I saw beautiful music
As I watched the Moon
Eclipsed by Earth's shadow
And dancing stars, shimmering
Against a crystal midnight sky.
A simple melody, clear, symphonic—
And I watched two stars faint dead away
From sheer joy.

Tonight I heard beautiful music
In the crackling accompaniment
Of the night's crawling creatures
Disturbing nature's carpet,
In the shrill cry of the silent-winged hunter
As clear and white as starlight
Floating gracefully.

Tonight I sang beautiful music
And was warmed clear to the soul
Watching each vaporous note
Dissipate into the crisp night air
To join the star dance
And the vanishing moon.

(Composed on the night of the eclipse in late 1993)

Night Sky

Starry, brilliant, shimmering sky
Backdrop of velvet so rich, so deep
Makes me wonder who am I
Gazing, counting, seeking sleep?

Diminished I am by the vastness of
This splendor aloft in glorious spray
Stretching far, beyond, above
The triviality of each day

Ursa, Canis, Orion can't say
Enough of the magnitude of the whole
These names we give do not convey
The breathless awe that fills my soul

Starry, starry magnificent sky
How might your stellar music sound?
Our swelling hearts would surely cry
To hear your song of joy abound

~ ~ ~ ~ ~

I agree with these words of Abraham Lincoln,
written when he was only 19 years old:

"I never behold the stars that I do not feel that I am
looking in the face of God. I can see how it might be
possible for a man to look down upon the earth and be
an atheist, but I cannot conceive how he could look up
into the heavens and say there is no God."

Kidstuff

Our Cats

Your cat is smart
Your cat is furry
Your cat is never
In a hurry

My cat is dumb
My cat is hairless
But -- just like yours
My cat could care less

Cherubunny

A bunny is an angel
With its wings misplaced:
Instead of on its back,
They were put near its face.

Bobcat

Lily had a funny cat
His name was Bob
And he was fat.

He had 3 legs,
His tail was bent,
She took him
Everywhere she went.

He liked the car,
He liked the bus,
He traveled well,
He was no fuss.

One day she took him
On a boat
That day she learned
That Bob could float.

He saw a fishy
Swimming by
He dove right in--
And that is why

He'll never ride
A boat again,
He gets his fishies
From a can.

What's Your Favorite Color?

Green, green,
Oh, I really like green!
It reminds me of grass
And growing things!
And frogs and lizards
And apples in the fall
Yes, I like green the best of all.

No, wait, it's blue,
Yes, blue is for me!
Like the bright sky above
And the deep blue sea
And the swimming pool
And my brand new bike
Yes, it's blue, that's what I like!

I forgot about red!
Like the deep red rose
And the big fire engine
That howls when it goes
And yummy strawberries
And watermelon each summer
Red is the one, there can be no other!

Oh me and oh my!
Now, what about yellow!
Like the sun, that warm
And shiny fellow
And bananas and lemons
The daffodil and daisy
So many choices just drive me crazy!

Okay, then, okay
Here is my problem
I can't choose just one
"Cause I like all of 'em
And purple and white
Orange, brown and pink
And teal and black
They all make me think

What a fantastic work
That God has done,
He made enough colors
For everyone!

Do you know these colors?

Magenta, celadon, violet, coral
Fuchsia, lavender, cream, cobalt
Burgundy, tan, mauve, ochre
Beige, sienna, rust, vermillion
Aqua, gold, cerise, bronze
Cinnamon, lilac, goldenrod, ecru
Indigo, maroon, ivory, jade
Khaki, taupe, olive, periwinkle
Chartreuse, sepia, grey, salmon

Blubbercraft

He took her to the beach with him
To see if his fat dog could swim
Short and fat and close to the ground
He needed to know if she would drown

She had no fear of water and sand
She didn't run for high and dry land
She stepped right in up to her belly
And chased that creature made of jelly

From bow to stern and fore to aft
That dog was a classic blubbercraft
Her feet left the sand and she was afloat
Like a bobbing little doggy boat

No more does her owner have concern
Of losing his dog in a tidal churn
He'll let her romp and chase and play
In the happiness of ocean spray

The Habit

Once in the habit
    Of keeping a rabbit,
        You'll never be able to break it
            (the habit).

Once your rabbit
    Knows of your habit,
        Wherever you go, you must take it
            (the rabbit).

22

Food for Thought

Shannon's hamster
Likes the wheel
He spins about all day
Then stops to rest his dizzy head
And nibble on some hay

If I go out
And ride fast rides
And spin and flip about
Then try to nibble on a treat
What goes in soon comes out

What does Shannon's hamster know
That makes his food stay and not go?

My Cat Is A Lyin' Dog

She'll purr and pretend
You're her dearest friend,
She can be so sweet
Till it's time to eat,
Then she's off your lap
And on her feet—
    My cat is a lyin' dog.

    My cat, my cat
    My big fat cat
    My cat is a lyin' dog.

She also pretends
That you're *not* her friend,
She can skillfully ignore you,
Whatever room you're in.
She knows we heard that cat fight,
But she fakes like she was in—
    My cat is a lyin' dog.

    My cat, my cat
    My big fat cat
    My cat is a lyin' dog.

She'll bug you to death
If you're the first one up,
Till you're forced to feed that mouth
Just to make it shut up,
Then she'll beg from all who follow,
Like a starvin' pup—
    My cat is a lyin' dog.

    My cat, my cat
    My big fat cat
    My cat is a lyin' dog.

Don't be taken in
By this furry friend,
Who lies next to her dish
Like her life's at an end,
This is acting at its best
As she puts you to the test—
     My cat is a drama queen.

     My cat, my cat
     My big fat cat
     My cat is a lyin' dog.

Make no quick moves
Towards the kitchen,
Or you'll see that tail
Begin a-twitchin',
And she's underfoot
Before you can start...countin'—
     My cat is a hungry hog.

     My cat, my cat
     My big fat cat
     My cat is a lyin' dog.

A purrfectly deceitful,
Conniving cat—
My cat is a lying' dog.

Mrs. Talley's Rats

The rats were thick back in the alley
Behind the home of Mrs. Talley.

They ate her food, they crawled through walls,
They chewed holes in her crocheted shawls.

She called the landlord, she called the city,
She found no one who showed her pity.

She didn't know what else to do,
She tried to kill them with her shoe.

One day she called the local Pound
They said 'Come see us, come on down.'

And so she went to search and see
What beast could help with her alley.

She thought about that vicious dog
Who growled and chewed upon a log.

But Mrs. Talley soon was smitten
By the tender mewing of a starving kitten.

She brought him home, she fed him well,
And in a few months, his belly swelled.

As soon as he was looking good,
Mrs. Talley stopped his food.

She put him out one night so black,
And told him he could not come back.

Until he learned to feed himself,
She bought no cat food for her shelf.

He stayed away for fifteen days,
Then home he came with eyes ablaze.

He was quite plump and round and fat,
He'd developed quite a taste for rat.

She named him Poison, that smart Mrs. Talley,
Who found a way to clean up her alley.

My Doggy

My doggy loves his food
He eats more than he should
    My doggy is a hoggy

My doggy likes to keep cool
He loves our swimming pool
    My doggy is soggy

My doggy loves to play
He runs around all day
    My doggy is groggy

Family

Erin

Erin is a pixie girl
With pixie grin
And pixie curl.
She'll cast her spell
And you'll never know,
'Til your heart is in a whirl.

Be careful of her
Big-eyed boys,
I'm warning you right now.
You'll want to give her
All your toys
And make that sacred vow.

She's fair of face,
How bright those eyes!
She has a cunning wit.
Look out!
She'll take you by surprise!
Take my advice and git!

Don't look too deep
Into those eyes,
And don't return her grin.
For once you do
The bait's been took—
She'll quickly reel you in.

For Erin is a pixie girl
With pixie grin
And pixie curl.
And once her silky web is spun—
It's much too late to run!

Dead Men Don't....

His face was still and lifeless
Like I've never seen it before
The form resembled my loved one indeed
But I really was quite unsure

The mouth had fallen open
The brow had lost its stress
Such peace surrounded this motionless man
At his horizontal rest

I leaned in for a better glimpse
Then came an alarming ROAR!
I knew right away that this stiff was mine
For dead men just don't snore!!

The Fight Begins Downstairs

The fight begins downstairs
Then up a flight it goes
While fists and curses fly
Along with shoes and clothes

Brothers on each other
In constant competition
Fighting is so natural
With daily repetition

Yet they'll defend each other
If you think neither cares
Just lay a finger on one and
The fight begins downstairs

Kenn(y)eth

He didn't like his nickname,
We couldn't call him Kenny.
Each time we did that boy would charge
Each one of us a penny.

He held his ground as he grew up,
We fell on harder times:
Inflation and that nickname stole
Our quarters and our dimes.

That boy got shrewder in his teens,
And we were pressing our luck,
Say the wrong thing, use the nickname—
That boy was taking our buck!

The Last Laugh?

Mr. C did not feel well,
The pain was in his back.
He twisted, squirmed, he tossed and turned,
But those bones just would not crack

Mrs. C was trying to sleep,
But his pain she hoped to ease.
She flung the covers fast away
And rolled onto her knees.

He gladly turned onto his chest
While she kneaded, pushed and prodded.
She punched, massaged and squeezed his back,
But the pain – she could not dislodge it.

Nothing moved, she heard no pop,
She flopped back down in the sack.
Her husband sighed 'it just might help
If you walk upon my back.'

'I'm game to try!' She laughed and then
She stood upon the bed.
It was the last laugh for Mrs. C,
As the ceiling fan blade struck her head.

That caring wife gave not one thought
To the ceiling that was so low,
Or the rapidly spinning fan above
That delivered the fatal blow.

She only thought to help her mate
Who, in his pain, did distract her.
Her insurance eased his pain quite well,
He's now dating his new chiropractor.

Kyle

I have a nephew, name of Kyle,
A very handsome lad.
He has his father's winning smile—
A chip off the old dad.

He has the role of oldest
And the only son, to boot.
But I, his aunt, still pinch his cheeks
And tell him he is cute.

But all too soon he's grown, this Kyle,
And gone his boyish curl.
One day he'll flash that winning smile
At an unsuspecting girl.

Connecting with Corey

How I long to remove the rage
That's etched upon his boyish brow
Unclench the fists so tight and tense
And smooth the lips shaped in a scowl

This child a pawn, a chess game piece
Jerked constantly between two homes
Addicted parents in selfish war
Then both disappear, the pawn is alone

So Corey moves to foster homes
One, then two, now ours makes four
He can't relax or trust or feel
Or hope for more than a swinging door

We work to earn his trust each day
Gently, firmly, helping him grow
Challenging him to forgive and detach
From the depths of pain his soul must know

Thanksgiving Day

There's a lamb in the kitchen
Knocking biscuits to the floor
And she's prancing, hopping, bleating
As we chase her out the door

There's a turkey in the oven
And the guests are due at noon
Old Auntie's started smiling
As she licks the batter spoon

The leaves have started drifting
As the wind whips in the snow
The little critters scurry
To their warm and earthy holes

Our Grandpa's outside herding
Cows and sheep and horses in
Mom is fetching Sammy home
From playing with his best friends

We set up several tables
To make room for everyone
And pull out cards and dominoes
For the after dinner fun

Tantalizing aromas
And the weather make me smile
Anticipating family
That we've not seen for a while

Thanksgiving Day has started
And we're all so thankful for
The gifts of God we all share
In our farmhouse near the shore

The Prize

"Have you been digging in the yard?"
She cried with great alarm.
I backed away, now on my guard,
But she swiftly grabbed my arm.
Her angry eyes burned into me,
I choked a gulp of fear,
Too late– she quickly grabbed my prize
And used it on my rear.

The prize that brought about such pain
Was ancient, priceless, rare!
The archaeologist I was
Could see 'twas beyond compare.
The wooden thing unearthed by me
(Within her sacred beds
Of flowers tended carefully)
Put madness in my head.

Was it Egyptian, from the tomb
Of a famous king or prince?
Or useful tool, utensil, toy
Handcrafted by Indians?
And so it was while I was lost
In my imagination,
I paid that very tender cost
For my digging violation.

Seems all that I had found that day
(Once jarred back to my senses),
Was probably just tossed away
Or lost by previous tenants.
A modern wooden paddle toy
(Without stretchy string and ball)
Was only dirty garbage now
With no prize value at all.

While ordinary it might have been
The thing possessed some power;
An unexplained phenomenon
Occurred that very hour.
That relic, I believe, was cursed,
And laid in soil so fine,
Just waiting for me to suffer
The affect on my bottom line!

(A true story, dedicated to my Green Thumb Mom!)

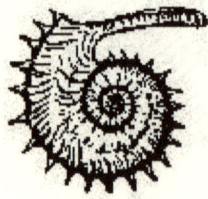

Love

A Summer's Farewell

Think of me as your face is brushed
By the gentle ocean breeze,
And as it softly sweeps through palms
And rustles all the leaves.

Think of me as you ride those waves
From sea to ocean shore;
And as you doze in a beach chair nap
And wake to your own snore.

Think of me as your skin turns brown
From the California rays,
And how I'll admire your beachy look
And fill your ears with praise.

Think of me as you walk the beach
In casual, skimpy clothes,
And as the sand and water join
To squish between your toes.

On second thought, it's probably best
If your thoughts are left undone -
You won't have time to think of me,
You'll be having too much fun!

Untitled

(Author Unknown–
 a favorite poem from the early 1970s)

I climbed the door
And shut the stairs.
I said my shoes
And took off my prayers.
I shut out the bed
And climbed into the light.
And all because he kissed me
Goodnight.

Song of Seth

Softly softly whispering leaves
Lilting song of the gentle breeze
Calling to my melancholy
Luring me into love's folly

Sunlight kisses verdant meadow
Dotted dandelion yellow
There he waits amid bee humming
Anticipates the romance coming

Twittering birds in happy flight
Steal my arrival from his sight
In forest shade I catch my breath
Then run to fill my arms with Seth.

My Sonnet

I wonder about fissures, cracks and breaks—
What causes them and why some do divide,
And why a stream should choose the fork it takes,
To be a narrow ford or river wide?
And when I see a window or a dish
Containing evidence in whole or part
Of some mistake or accident, I wish
I could repair the fracture in your heart.
It takes great skill and patience, so I'm told,
To listen well and try to ascertain
The spring, the root, the source of grief untold,
And search to find the origin of pain.
    And yet I'm certain to my very core,
    That I can heal your heart to love once more.

Lost Love

There comes a time amidst the rush and hurry,
When we must force ourselves to a grinding halt,
So as not to miss the moment, the event, the beauty—
And then regret our own preoccupied fault.

Overtaken by all we think important,
We forget that we must weigh the value of
A small time-fragment willingly expended,
To spare the grief and misery of lost love.

The Goodbye Kit

The Q-Tips are a reminder
That you always have my ear
The tissues are here just in case
Our parting brings a tear

The Kisses show my affection
And I have so much for you;
The chocolate is required
For the days you're feeling blue.
(AND, of course, we know it's good
For happy moments, too!)

The mirror holds an image of
The one I hold so dear.
Look upon it knowing that
My love is very near.

The red hots should remind you
Of the Arizona heat,
The candy scorpion simply means
No more stingers in your feet!

I hope that all these little things
Will bring you grins and smiles.
Remember the distance between us
Is only a matter of miles.

Outrageous Expectations

A knight in dripping armor
Came forth to rescue me,
Dismounted from his seahorse,
Limped out of the foaming sea.

His armor was quite rusted,
He didn't have a sword.
With helmet visor busted,
He looked unkempt and bored.

Was this my handsome future?
Where was the noble steed?
How could this one protect me
And furnish every need?

My hopefulness receded
Like waves along the shore,
My childhood dream eroded
Until it was no more.

To Your Heart

If Life should cut me a new deck of cards,
And deal me a new hand to play,
I don't think I'd find things quite so hard—
I'd know all the right words to say.

My thoughts, my actions, the roads that I'd seek
Would never be left to chance.
The use of my time, the company I'd keep—
By choice, not coincidence.

Yet though I believe that great changes I'd make
In Life as it so far has been,
The road to Love I'd assuredly take
Would lead to your heart once again.

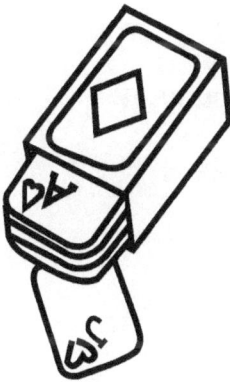

The Wind Doesn't Care

Fallen pods of palo verde tree
Scattered randomly in dust around me
Brown and brittle
Cracking open
Like my heart
Searing summer sun
Scorches my hair
But the wind doesn't care

Pain like the scorpion's sting
Swollen, throbbing, fevered thing
Red radial lines
Pointing to
Infected heart
Sweltering thunderstorm
Builds to monsoon
But the wind doesn't care

Love found legs, walked away
Tears refuse me first time today
Busy, pecking birds
Disregard me
Like his heart
Sweating, snorting horses
Kick up dust into
The wind that doesn't care

Without . . .

A ripened peach without the fuzz
A busy bee without a buzz
A happy dog without a tail
A corkscrew shell without a snail

A hungry cat with no meow
A dairy farm without a cow
A briny lobster without a claw
A rousing hee without a haw

A chugging train without a track
A dromedary with no humpback
A redneck man without a truck
A sparkling pond without a duck

A hurricane without an eye
A hot, summer day without a fly
A lightning storm without a strike
A politician without a mike

Have you caught the drift
Of each silly clue?
There just can't be a Me
Without a You!

Faith

Little Things

Waking up each day
Again defying death
Yawning, stretching, yawning
Taking yet another breath
Bending, reaching for the paper
In its carelessly-tossed place
The early warmth of sunshine or
Bite of winter on my face.
Thank you, Lord, for all these little things.

Comforting aromas
Greet me all day through
Electricity
For all the things I do
Toilets, bathtubs and showers
The plumbing rarely lets me down
Internet and email sometimes
Make me smile and frown
Thank you, Lord, for all these little things

Pure loyalty and joy
From my precious pets
Walking to the mailbox
In my favorite sweats
Waving to neighbors waving back
Loading kids into their vans
Sounds of laughter, clapping
From enthusiastic weekend fans
Thank you, Lord, for all these little things

Chatting with family
Even if it's quick
Envelopes and stamps
That do not need a lick

Hearing consistent breathing
From my deeply sleeping spouse
Sitting alone in the peacefulness
Of my late-night silent house
Thank you, Lord, for all these little things

Lord, I'm thankful for your presence
In the big things in my life
Houses, jobs, kids and college,
And being a godly wife
I love your flowers and sunsets,
And every bird that sings
But I'm also thankful, Lord,
That you are there in little things.

Recognition

I hear You calling from afar
And yet my ears do not discern
The Shepherd's voice known to His sheep
This stubborn lamb has much to learn.

I know You speak from deep inside
Called intuition or gut instinct
That Voice is the filter, our moral guide
To keep us on course and off the brink.

But most times, Lord, I need to hear
Your voice in deafening frequencies
Capturing my attention loud and clear
Like hurricane winds that toss the trees.

You speak in creative, cosmic ways
Simple it should be to open my ears
And yes, my heart and soul and mind
To know Your will and quell my fears.

But I let distractions daily drown
What I most need to comprehend
I rarely turn the world's noise down
To hear the messages You send.

You're lovingly calling every day
Inside my routine, my job, my car
In music, nature, a child's sweet play
But recognition's incredibly hard.

Of course, mistaken is what I've been
Your voice is not like a distant star
You're always as close, Lord, as my skin
It's me who drifts often and afar.

I hear You calling, You're very near
Whispering soft as a gentle breeze
Speaking words I need to hear
To bring me humbly to my knees.

John 10:4: "...he goes before them, and the sheep follow him because they know his voice."

Mercy on the Menu

Countless choices choke us
With each recurring day
Do this, do that, do this again
In twenty different ways
Conveniences are endless
No need to think or do
Yet mercy's always waiting there
For us on God's menu

Mercy on the menu
When we can't sort out the day
Our chain can't be unknotted
And our mouth gets in the way
He offers us forgiveness
And love beyond compare
Through days of pain and times of peace
His mercy's always there

Shades of gray exist
In decisions black and white
The media distorts the truth
Confusing wrong with right
Those whom we've elected
Build us up and let us down
Oil prices fluctuate
And make our heads spin round

But mercy's on the menu
To guide us through our day
To break the chain once knotted
Provide wise words to say
He offers us forgiveness
And love beyond compare
We only need to ask Him
His mercy's always there

God's Love For Me

I cannot know the breadth of your love
With no defined borders for me to see
My arms can't expand enough to display
Just how much you truly love me.

I cannot grasp the length of your love
It encompasses distances beyond my view
There is no horizon, beginning nor end
Of the love I receive from you.

I cannot reach the height of your love
It stretches to heaven so infinitely
Yet every moment of every day
You bend down and give it to me.

I cannot probe the depth of your love
So unfathomable, bottomless, vast
I cannot measure nor penetrate this
Profound love that covers my past.

Ephesians 3:14-19

He Works Out At My Gym

I think I'll never cease to marvel
At the many ways
And lengths that God will go to
Just to speak to me some days.

And if I try to run and hide and
Get away from Him,
I just can't get too far at all--
He reaches me at the gym.

Some of those manly muscled men,
When they start to flex,
Will flaunt their artistic tattoos
And that's when I start to vex.

A scripture reference on an arm,
Meant for me to see--
When I get home and look it up,
It's a message from God to me!

Humility

It's most unwise
In our Father's eyes
To compare your woes
With the sufferings of those
You encounter every day.

My difficulties
To you are a breeze,
While her smooth sailing
Could set him to wailing--
We process things in our own way.

Keep that in mind
When your words start to grind,
You've no call to judge
Or even begrudge
The life of your neighbor or friend.

In life's grand game,
God loves us the same.
So let each problem
Draw you *to* Him--
He'll carry you through to the end.

Country

The Warrior

Too-soon dawns greet bleary eyes
Etched in pain that fail to disguise
Treacherous journeys faced each day
Restless nights fall hard and stay
The warrior trudges on

Clear battle lines cannot be drawn
As boundaries shift, are trampled on
By those who once resembled friends
Then morphed to foes and bitter ends
The warrior trudges on

Unhinged he's not, by wounds of wars
And countless surface battle scars
With psyche sound in weary head
His aching bones he takes to bed
The warrior trudges on

Marching, stumbling tirelessly
Unchallenged by geography
Rocky crags or forest greens
Seamy landscapes few have seen
The warrior trudges on

The taste of fear, it lingers on
It haunts him like an ancient song
It fuels him, he has felt its sting
He's known the loss of everything
The warrior trudges on

The goal, the prize, the golden ring
An undefined, ethereal thing
Within the heart the answer rests
What this traveler must possess
The warrior trudges on

How Red The Waves

How red the waves that lap the shore
And stir the tumbled grains of sand
Where lifeless lay our gallant young
Whose shoulders national honor bore

Where fall the tears, Americans,
For every patriotic soul?
Such noble loss so you can be
Distracted by your hollow plans

Wake up, O Youth who live today
Without a thought of those before
Nor conscious of the future debt
For carelessly giving our country away

Uneasy Silence
(The Battle of Iwo Jima, Feb. 1945)

The lull, the end of violence
Their eyes dart everywhere
The dread, uneasy silence
Hangs so heavy in the air

The smoke is clearing, stretching thin
Loud echoes fade away
That pounding is their hearts again
First time discerned today

The lack of noise is deafening
They hardly dare to breathe
The silence just grows maddening
Their stations they won't leave

The stillness sweeps like rushing wind
Across the battlefield
The enemy has met its end
Their positions they can yield

Now audible, the moans are heard
The medics run to tend
To troops and loss so undeserved
And the stench of death again

A grossly miscalculated win
And the tragic stench of death again

Not Fallen

Don't let them be called 'the fallen'
The cherished ones we have lost
They didn't fall down in their duty—
A choice with enormous cost

Too dark and dismal, that label
Like Satan, who fell from God's grace
But not our soldiers, our champions
Who've gloriously died in our place

Raise high their lives, not their endings
They served us with pride, not regret
Preserving our treasured freedom—
We cannot afford to forget

Instead we honor, esteem, exalt
Our heroes who gave their last breath
We venerate all of our veterans
And revel in life, not death

Writing

Writer's Blight

Write Write Oh what shall I write
My mind is blank, it's writer's blight

Unless of course the problem is
My mind's too full of that and this

I'm just too afraid to sort it out—
If I open my mouth, my mind may shout

So my thoughts I'll keep and carefully hoard
Until they organize through my keyboard

Style

I wish sometimes that I could be
A poet who weaves gracefully
A texture rich in thought like those
Who pleasingly petal a page with prose.

How sweet to paint with words like 'splendor',
'Profound', 'undaunted', 'prophetic', to render
A work that's wholly worthy of
Honor, praise, admiration, love.

Long ago that man did lecture
Against my love of poetic structure.
'Release your mind, yes, set it free
To pen your thoughts more naturally.'

I strained, I groaned, I tried to force
My soul to find its natural course.
I had no clue, was not inspired,
I could not do what he required.

Tender my pride, I let it fester
But only for one vile semester.
Blind he was to what's true for me—
The rhyme is what comes naturally.

No, weaving splendor's not in my cards,
I'd rather join the merry bards
Who joyfully knit their words each time
With structure, meter, rhythm and rhyme.

Creative Surge

The pressure building inside one's head
Must be relieved to prevent brain dead
Bringing it out and writing it down
Like winning the prize, it will astound

Once the lush fountain begins to flow
The raging volcano starts to blow
One must be ready to capture it all
Every rich word and thought that falls

A trickle, a stream, a lava flood
The beat of life in the writer's blood
Grab the brilliance, substance, reason
Before the volcano's dormant season

Like the believer's path to a sweet forever
Wrought with potholes, debris, whatever
The end is worth a journey of pain
A trial by fire for precious gain

Life in General

Turning Over a New Leaf

I watched a leaf falling so gracefully,
It seemed as weightless as it could be.
It caught a light breeze, gently touched down,
And swiftly began inching across the ground.

That green leaf grew green legs before I could blink,
Crept back to the tree without once wavering,
Straight up the broad trunk, back out on a limb,
Launched itself into the breeze once again.

Over and over I witnessed this scene,
Then finally approached this leaf so enchanting.
Once it had landed, I nudged with my boot,
And saw a green lizard under leaf parachute.

My alarm was surprisingly held at bay,
I truthfully didn't know what to say,
I watched him again as he leapt from a branch,
Jabbering something about car insurance.

I backed away shaking my thick, muddled head,
Certain I'd soon wake up in my warm bed.
Instead, some commotion, a hullabaloo,
Some foolishness stirring in my backyard zoo!

My chickens were gathered along the link fence,
Tormenting the Guernsey with noise so intense,
But instead of cluck-clucking, I felt no relief
To hear them say "Got milk?" and
"Hey, where's the beef?"

The neighbor's old cow, usually sweet and serene,
Was acting quite mad now and looked scary-mean!
No, that wasn't lowing and mooing I heard:
"Chicken! Eat more chicken!" – were her very words.

My head was gyrating, legs wobbly and weak,
I lurched towards the house, too startled to speak.
I passed my two dogs, who looked perfectly sane
As they calmly discussed their high stakes poker game.

One leaping lizard
One very cross cow
Two little dogs that did not bark 'bow wow!'
Five bantering banty hens—
What's going on?
I'm losing my mind in the midday sun!

Why was this familiar? Not quite déjà vu...
But I couldn't process -- no, nothing came through;
I awoke at long last with a wail of a scream:
"No more late night TV with a side of ice cream!!"

Zzzzzzzzzzz...

My head is full of many things,
Heavy thoughts, old fears, new dreams,
Chores to do and those just done,
People to speak to,
Ways to have fun.

Sleep just does not easily come,
It's rough, elusive, quite undone,
Mind kicks in to overdrive
While counting sheep...
(9-0-4, 9-0-5...)

I need a switch just for my brain
To turn it off or let it drain,
So sleep can come just as it should,
And I'll make sounds
Like sawing wood!

What Mature Women Understand...

I feel the heat between us—
Is it passion? raw desire?
With all the pop and sizzle
Of an orangey-blue wood fire?

I know my pulse has quickened
Yes, my heart, I feel it racing
And such a warmth flows through me
Each time that we're embracing

Then comes the realization
The origin, the true heat cause
Was not anticipated—
Those vile flames of menopause.

You Know Who You Are

Cell phone permanently affixed to your ear
A conversation about nothing
Means you won't even hear
The teller, the clerk, perhaps a cashier,
You smugly think that they are all paid
To do your bidding, to serve and slave
You extend no courtesy, no eye contact made
Mindless chatter on wireless air waves
        You know who you are

Facts mean nothing in your selfish life
You have no firm foundation in truth
You'd rather gossip about so-and-so's wife
Such cruel, thoughtless acts, stirring up strife
To you it all seems to be a game
No effort required, no use of the brain
Has someone raised you to feel no shame?
To do what you want, disregard others' pain?
        You know who you are

How tender the hearts you tread upon
Undeserving of grief so absolute
You've not learned yet you're the tender one
That all you do is not about fun
You've not been dealt a losing card
Nor felt the pain you choose to give
One day life will hit you exceedingly hard
You'll have to discover how real people live
        Because you don't know who you are

Advice to New Students
(This style is called a Villanelle)

So now begins a long, tense year,
Perhaps made short because of school,
And professors view us with a sneer.

Tuition steals our pennies dear,
While the price of books could easily fuel
Our many friends -- in the form of beer.

All lines are long -- this is no stage;
It will not change, it is the rule.
You'll seek the exception in your rage.

Grades mean nothing, so have no fear.
In spite of all, the brain's the tool,
Though the greater strain is on your rear.

Knowledge is power, regardless of age,
Save the cream, all else is drool.
Develop your own reliable gauge.

Direct yourself, trust none to steer,
Let no one play you for the fool.
If you fall short when once so near—
Don't be afraid to shift the gear.

What Darkness

What darkness does her laughter mask
So deep within her soul,
Where sorrow dwells with pain more dense
Than anything we know?

Familial strife, a child is lost
Among divorce debris
Why can't the selfish weigh the cost
Of insensitivity?

Her crooked path needs straightening
And cleansing of all soot
Yet she creates more obstacles
So hope will not take root.

Her needs are love, stability,
Strong hands that wish to guide
Her to a place of trust and peace
To quell the angst inside.

What darkness can withstand attack
By this unwavering goal
To bring this lost one to the light
And save her tattered soul!

Memories of Daybreak

Cherish the blossoming Dawn!
While you are yet fresh and cherry-cheeked,
Serenading your phantom prince
On his splendid, golden moon
      Sing the gypsy's song.

While you can still frolic like an enchanted colt
Through rippling fields of dandelions and daisies,
And waltz among stately trees
With a butterfly's grace
      Dance the fairy's dance.

While waves of sleep can still transport you
To old creaking ships of young cavalier pirates,
And briny, bubbly kingdoms
Of lovely mermaids
      Sail the traveler's seas.

For soon your honey-petaled Day will wither
Into the long violet shadows of Dusk,
And your seasoned heart will yearn
For the precious whimsy of Morning
      When you dreamed the child's dream.

Free Bird

O to be that black bird
High atop the pepper tree
Balanced on the swaying branch
And gazing down at me

O to be above life
And the grime of roads and rails
To lose the grit between the toes
Beneath the fingernails

Soaring and ignoring
The harried and the hurried
The timelines and the deadlines
Feverish and flurried

A smile begins to turn
Up the corners of my mouth
The bird's a fine distraction from
This traffic snaking south

Admiringly I look at
This one who's eying me
Gladly I'd trade places with
That mockingbird so free

R.I.P.

Goodbye to all
Original thought
I shall not think again
Computers, machines
Do everything
No need to use the brain

I cannot add
Subtract and such
I need a calculator
Nor can I spell
Instead I text
I'm an abbreviator

Without my phone
I can't survive
I can't be disconnected
No matter what
No matter where
No call shall be rejected

I have no couth
Nor have I learned
Good manners or work ethic
I'm self-absorbed
Show no respect
I'll cut you off in traffic

Say adios
Farewell, so long
My words I shall not mince
We all should fear
Because it's here—
The death of common sense.

Daydream

Let your thoughts drift in and out
To places you love to dream about
Imagine a walk on distant shores
Removed from heartache, stress and chores

Feel the breeze as it tosses your hair
Enjoy a breathtaking scenery stare
Soak in the culture of foreign lands
Gather up treasures from pastel sands

And if your burdens tie you down
Preventing your mind from leaving town
Worldwide travel can be a sure bet
Just hitch a ride on the internet

Hidden Beauty

She stands behind the purple vase
A timid smile upon her face
Just barely seen between the stems
Of brilliantly-colored flowering gems

What might it be that plants her feet,
That stirs her heart to skip a beat?
A crush, a foe, a recurring fear?
Why does she hide and not come here?

We'll never know what spins inside
Her youthful head that she does hide
Nor hear someone call out her name—
She hangs on my wall in a wooden frame.

(Thoughts on a painting of the same name
by artist Barbara Wood)

A New Pet?

I once had a good friend named Daniel
Who desperately wanted a spaniel.
But his wife would not let him,
Instead she beget him
A strapping young son named Nathaniel.

Cutting Class

It should never ever be allowed,
That tedious time in-between,
Affording an attractive chance for escape
Without ever being seen.

With countless and diverse things to do,
Stairs or mountains to climb,
Boundless prospects for immediate action,
When left with far too much time.

Just one brief stop for a quick cup of hot,
Can become a luxurious retreat
Of relaxation too grand to resist—
A cup or two leads one to eat.

That time in-between is most deadly,
It's borderline precarious,
I know -- I've dealt with this before,
My reputation's nefarious.

The weight of decision is heavy—
Do what one wants or what's right?
And when one could easily go either way,
The tendency is always towards flight!

Elusive

It bounces in and kicks about
If I focus upon it, it bounces out

It does not stay, but leaves a trail
And I'll follow for hours to no avail

I strain brain cells to bring it back
But I pull up nothing, my rope's gone slack

What do I seek? That fleeting thought—
Which reappears when my search has stopped.

Nothing

Here's an insignificant rhyme
It will not take up any time
To read, and you'll soon ascertain,
It won't do much to rouse your brain.

You will not ponder, marvel, think
Nor push emotions to the brink
You won't desire to yell or sing
In truth, you won't feel anything.

You see?
What did I tell you, friend?
There's nothing here,
You've reached
The end.

Poems From My Youth

A collection of poems written when I was 13 years old....

...before we used computers...

...before white-out...

...before I even knew how to use...

(wait for it)

a typewriter*!!!

*Ask your grandparents what this is.

I Wonder…

I wonder what the future holds
For someone such as I.
It seems so near, it seems so far,
It will not pass me by.

Will life be then, as life is now—
An ever-changing scene?
Or will it finally settle down
To boring, dull, routine?

It seems that life, forever, is
A constant uphill climb.
The going is especially rough
For those who waste their time.

Just when you think you've reached the top
It's only just to find
A small plateau, a little rest,
Then up again you climb.

I think with all life's obstacles,
I'll never make it through.
And yet the future always comes,
No matter what we do.

I wonder what the future holds
For someone such as I.
It seems so near, it seems so far,
It will not pass me by.

A Flower Named Lee

There once was a Flower named Lee,
Who sun-bathed each nice day with glee.
Would an enemy attack,
He would bravely fight back,
But he always got stung - drat that Bee!

Poetry

Iambic, dactylic, anapestic, trochaic
They sounded so strange and so foreign
But as class time went by and we grudgingly learned
I found they were not all that borin'!

Rain

The rain falls
A mother calls
And bouncing balls
    Stop.

    Down it pours
    Against closed doors
    And outside chores
        Stop.

        A child complains
        Wants to be playing
        So finally the rain
            Stops!

The Mouse

One day as I was cleaning
Through the rooms inside my house,
I walked outside to get the broom:
Behind it was a mouse.

He peered at me so timidly,
He was so very small,
That, suddenly a giant,
I felt ninety-two feet tall.

His small gray frame was ragged and frail,
Poor hunger-stricken soul;
He'd probably tried to get some crumbs
From Kitty's empty bowl.

As eye to frightful eye we stared,
A thought occurred to me,
This same thing (from our fellowman)
Do not we often see?

Starving people, homeless ones,
And wretched poverty;
Yet they are real live people,
Just like you and me.

If every man would help to meet
The problems of today,
I think one day I'd look to find
My mouse has gone away.

www.ingramcontent.com/pod-product-compliance
Lightning Source LLC
LaVergne TN
LVHW092318080426
835509LV00034B/844

* 9 7 8 0 6 1 5 2 5 7 0 3 7 *